READABOUT
Measurement

© 1992 Franklin Watts

Franklin Watts
96 Leonard Street
London EC2A 4RH

Franklin Watts Australia
14 Mars Road
Lane Cove
NSW 2066

UK ISBN: 0 7496 0857 9

A CIP catalogue record for this book
is available from the British Library

Editor: Ambreen Husain
Design: K and Co

Printed in Hong Kong

Additional photographs:
ZEFA pp 12 and 13

READABOUT

Measurement

Text: Henry Pluckrose
Photography: Chris Fairclough

Franklin Watts
London/New York/Sydney/Toronto

There are some things
you need to know...
like the size of shoe
you wear.

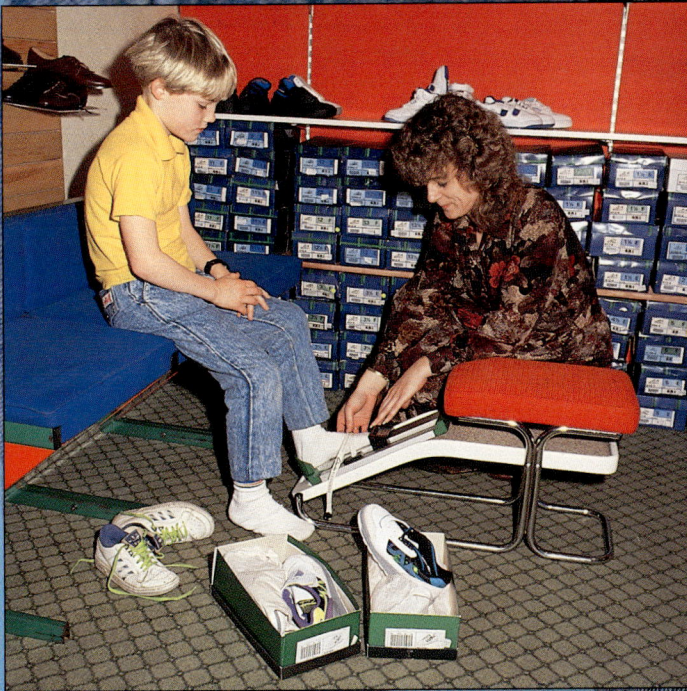

You can have your feet measured.
The measure gives the length and width of each foot.

When you buy clothes
they should fit you.
The numbers on the labels
give the sizes.

St·Michael®

MADE IN MAURITIUS

AGE	TO FIT CHEST
5-6	23in

TOUR DE POITRINE
58cm

MADE IN
HONG KONG
16"-41CM

Do you know
what size you are?

We use numbers to measure.
We need something else too.
How long is the toy car?
It is **8** centimetres long.
The centimetre is
a measure of length.

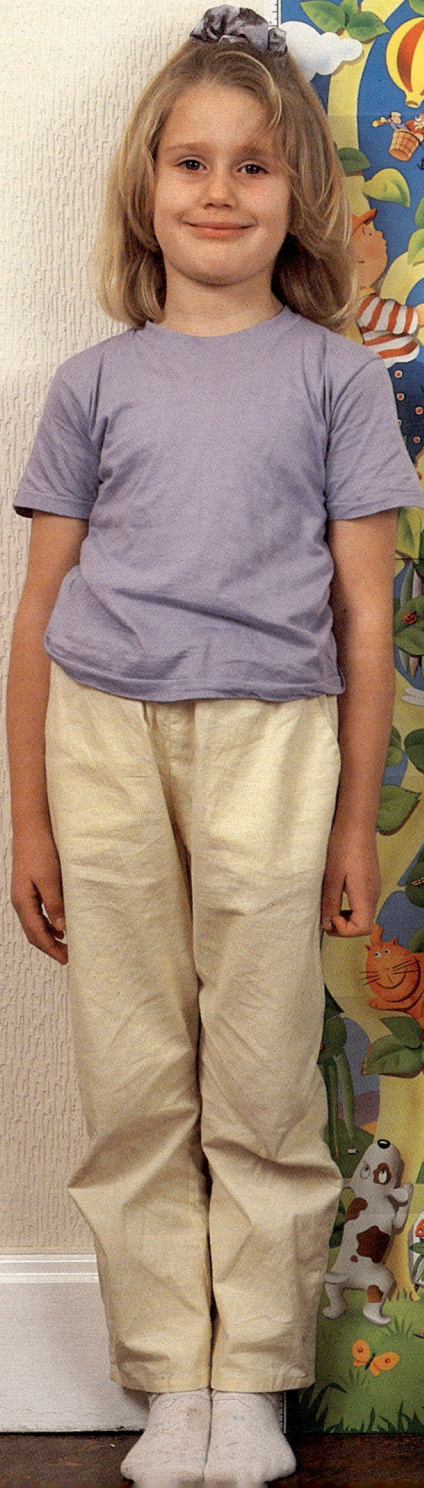

You can also measure
your height in centimetres.
How tall are you?

Centimetres are useful
for measuring small lengths.
It would be difficult
to measure this tennis court
in centimetres.

You could use a metre stick,
a tape
or a click wheel.
How many centimetres
make one metre?

Niederhöchstadt

Frankfurt a. M. 14 km
Frankfurt a. M. 🛣

Niederhöchstadt
Ortsteil West

The kilometre is 1,000 metres. It is used in many countries to measure long distances.

ΕΠΙΣΚΟΠΕΙΟΝ
Episkopio 3M

ΠΕΡΑ
Pera 4M

ΨΗΜΟΛΟΦΟΥ
Psomolophou 5M

ΠΑΛΑΙΧΩΡΙ
Palekhori 14M

ΑΓΡΟΣ
Agros 23M

ΛΕΥΚΩΣΙΑ
Nicosia 14M

In some countries, long distances are measured in miles.

When you are ill
your temperature is taken.
A thermometer is used
to find out
whether you are hot
and feverish.

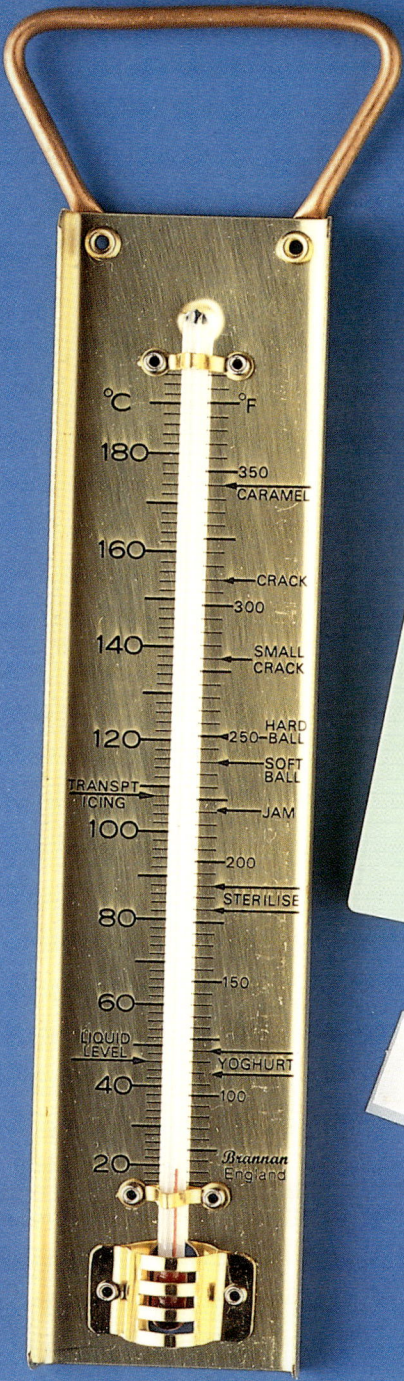

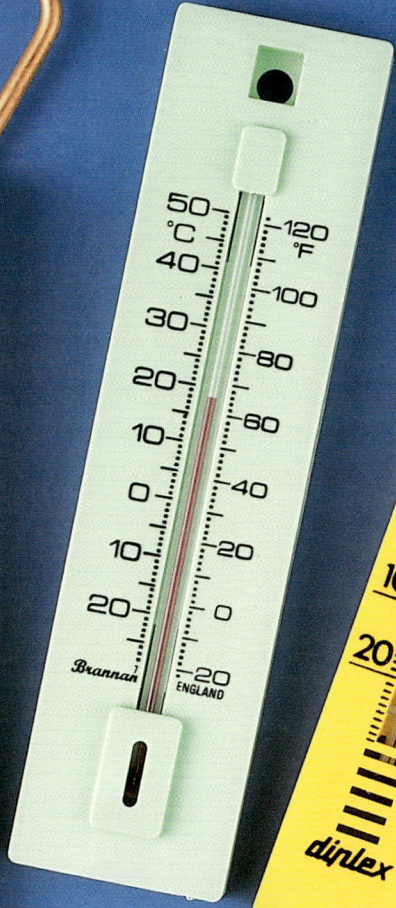

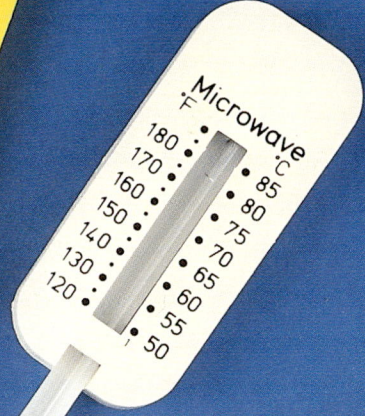

The thermometer gives your temperature.
It measures heat.
Where would you find these thermometers?

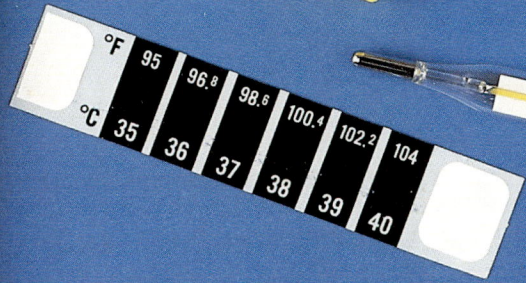

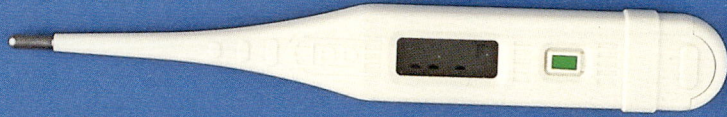

We need to be able to measure
in other ways.
You can not take a temperature
with a ruler...

or buy potatoes by the metre.

We need to be able to measure
how heavy things are.
This scale weighs things
which are very light.

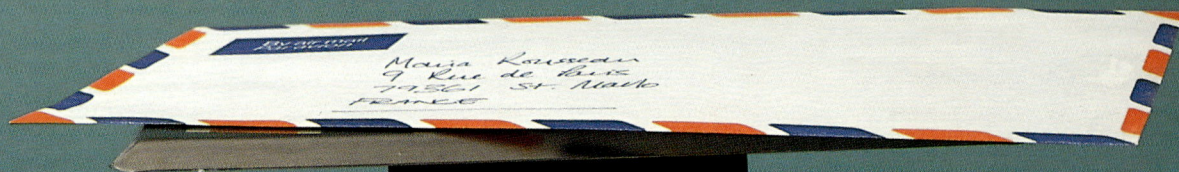

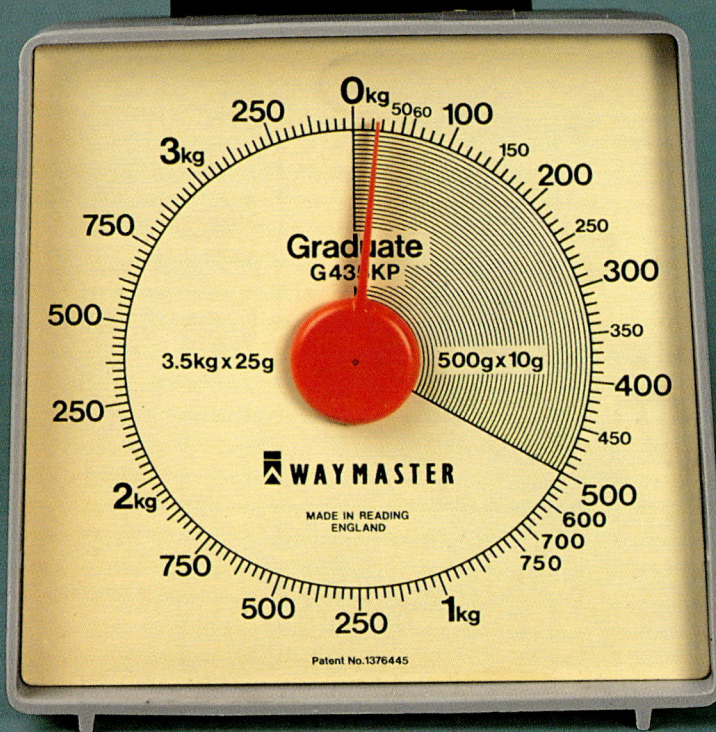

Scales like these are used
for weighing food.
The kilogram weight
balances the kilogram of apples.
The kilo is a measure of weight.

Here are some more scales
and balances.
What kind of things could you
weigh on them?

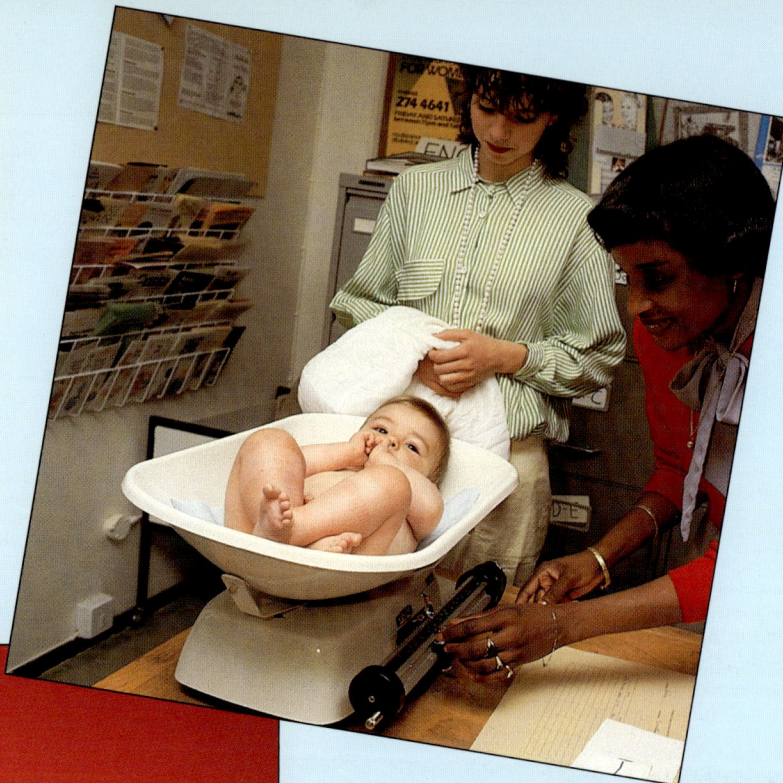

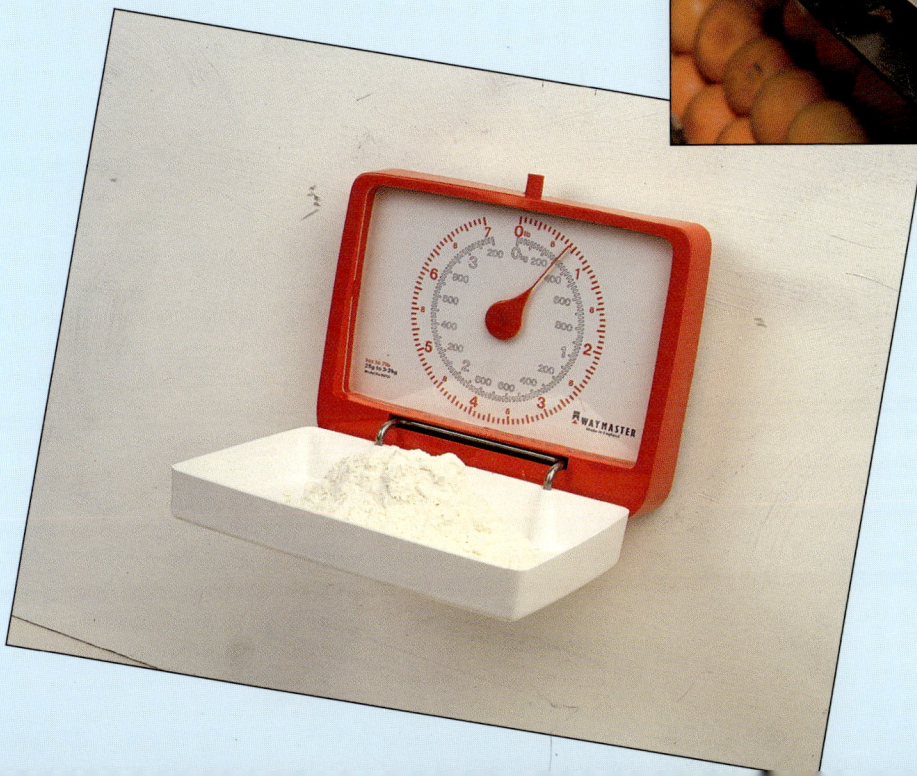

Sometimes we measure things
by the space they fill...
a cup of flour,
a spoonful of coffee,
a scoop of ice cream,
a handful of sweets,
a bowl of cereal.

But some things are difficult
to measure.

We can tell how much water
we have by measuring
the space that it fills.
This jug measures one litre.

MILLILITRES   FLOZ. PINTS

1100 — — 40 — 2

1 LITRE — — 35 1¾

900 — — 30 1½

800 —

700 — — 25 1¼

600 — — 20 1

½ LITRE —

400 — — 15 ¾

APPROXIMATE MEASURES

300 — — 10 ½

200 —

  — 5 ¼

100 —

A litre of water fills
the same amount of space
as a litre of juice
or a litre of milk.
We use litres to measure volume.
Volume is the space inside
a container.

These containers each hold one litre –
even though each has a different shape.

**What can be measured
using these?
Where would you find them?**

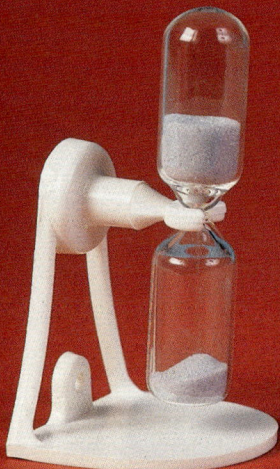

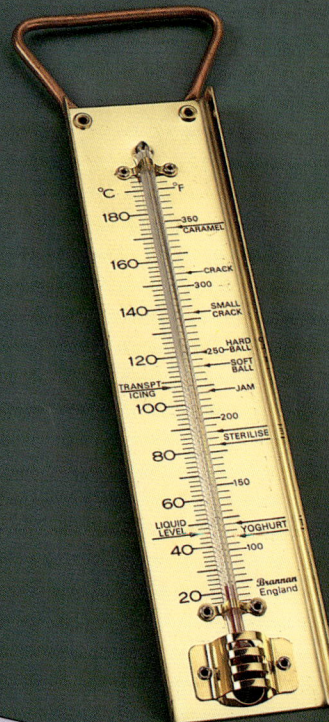

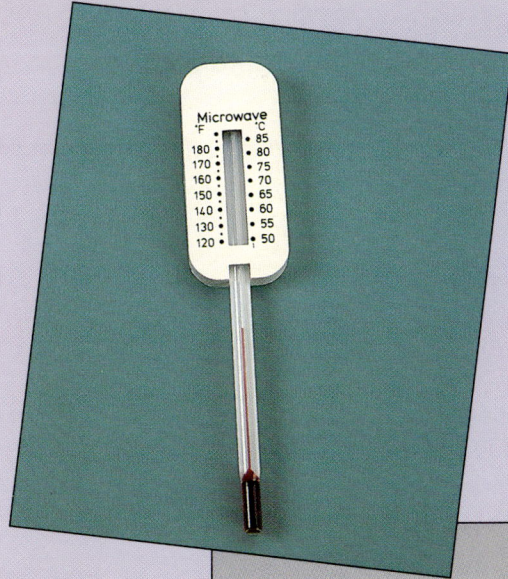

Almost everything can be measured.
How many different ways could you measure these things?

How many things can you measure about yourself?

About this book

All books which are specially prepared for young children are written to meet the interest of the age group at which they are directed. This may mean presenting an idea in a humorous or unconventional way so that ideas which hitherto have been grasped somewhat hazily are given sharper focus. The books in this series aim to bring into focus some of the elements of life and living which we as adults tend to take for granted.

This book develops and explores an idea using simple text and thought-provoking photographs. The words will encourage questioning and discussion – whether they are read by adult or child. Children enjoy having information books read to them just as much as stories and poetry. The younger child may ignore the written words…pictures play an important part in learning, particularly if they encourage talk and visual discrimination.

Young children acquire much information in an incidental, almost random fashion. Indeed, they learn much just by being alive! The adult who uses books like this one needs to be sympathetic and understanding of the young child's intellectual development. It offers a particular way of looking, an approach to questioning which will result in talk, rather than "correct" one word answers.

Henry Pluckrose